Triceratops

The fierce **Triceratops** (try-SER-a-tops) was a tank-sized creature who looked like a frilly-collared rhinoceros. Its frilly collar was actually solid bone that protected its neck from flesh-eating dinosaurs. The triceratops was an aggressive animal, and because it was so well defended by its bony armor and sharp horns, it had no real enemies. Its skull was over 7 feet long. This plant-eater roamed in great herds in what is now western North America and was one of the last of the dinosaurs to become extinct.

Stegosaurus

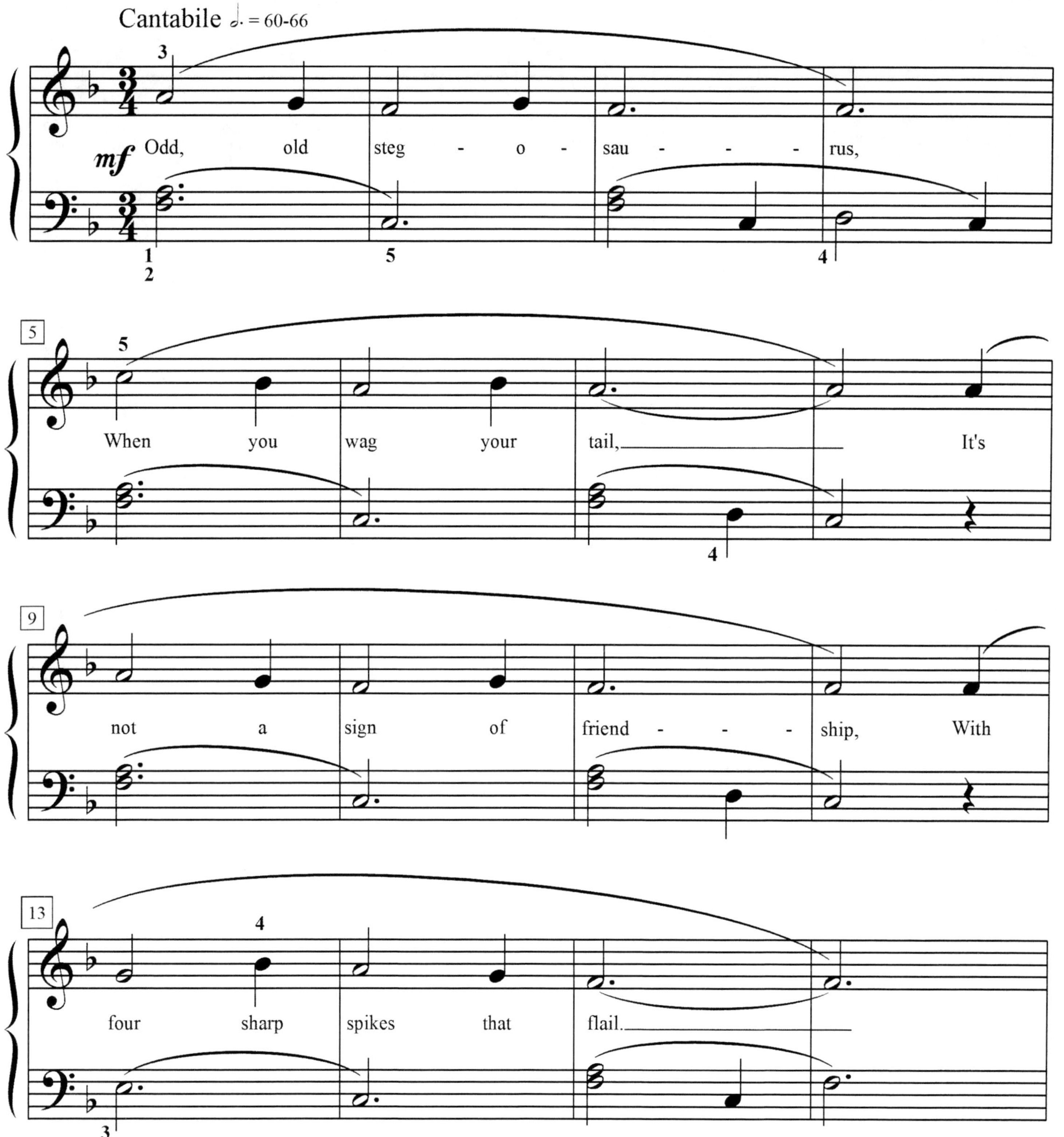

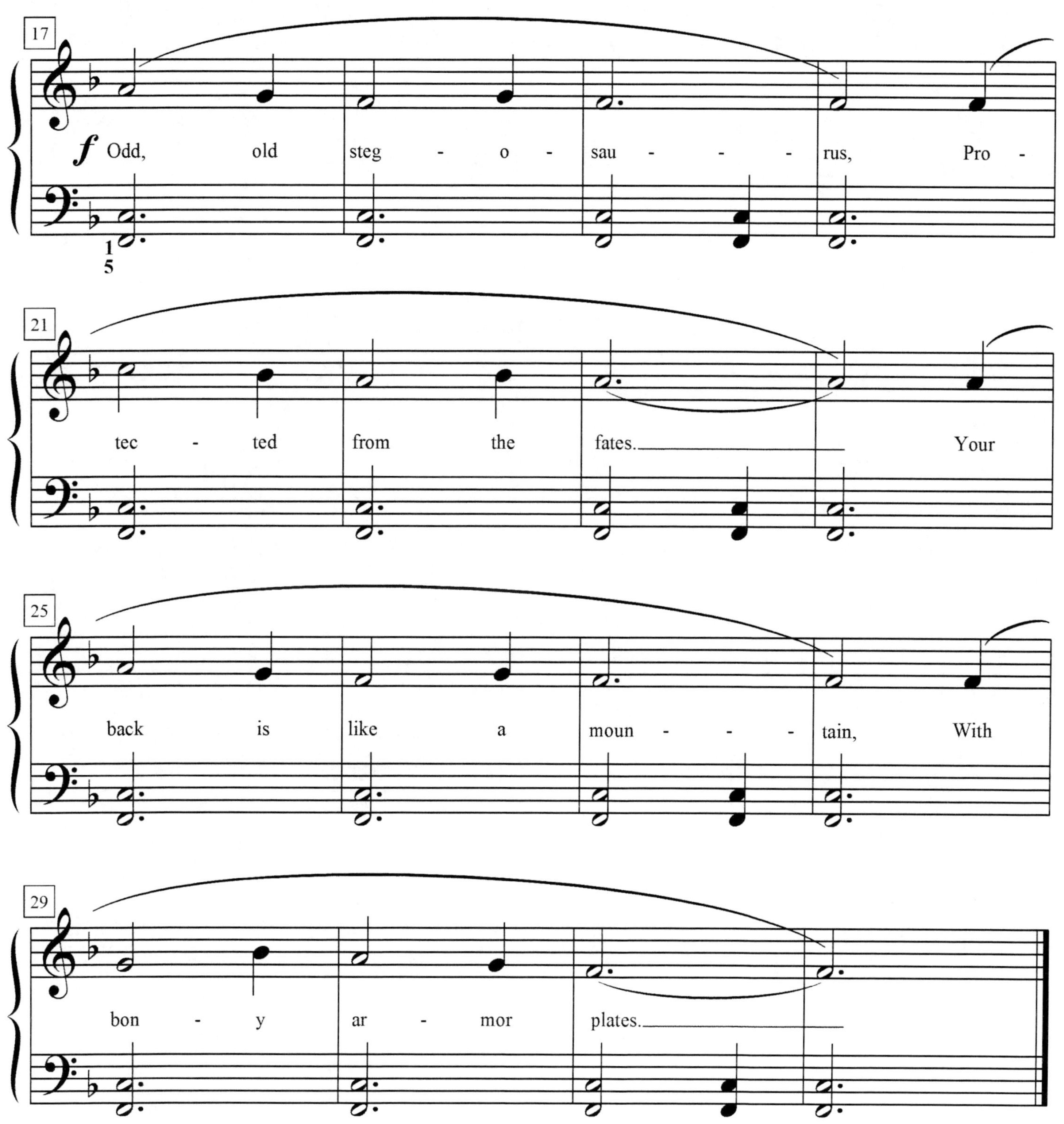

The **_Stegosaurus_** (steg-o-SAWR-us), meaning "plated lizard," had rows of bony plates running down his back. He is the only plated dinosaur ever discovered in North America. Although the stegosaurus was as big as an elephant, he had a small head, a small beak-like mouth and a brain the size of a golf ball. He was a plant eating dinosaur that roamed the ancient swamps of Colorodo and Wyoming. He could defend himself from flesh-eating dinosaurs by swinging his tail, with its four sharp, bony spikes.

Ankylosaurus

The **Ankylosaurus** (an-kih-lo-SAWR-us) had thick skin that was covered with bony armor and spikes, keeping it safe from almost all of its enemies. Its name means "armored lizard." It could also defend itself with its large bony tail that could swing like a club. It was really a peaceful plant-eating dinosaur that grew to a length of 25 feet and weighed about 5 tons. Gulping down its food in large chunks, it often slept for two weeks! Along with triceratops, it was one of the last dinosaurs to die out.

Elasmosaurus

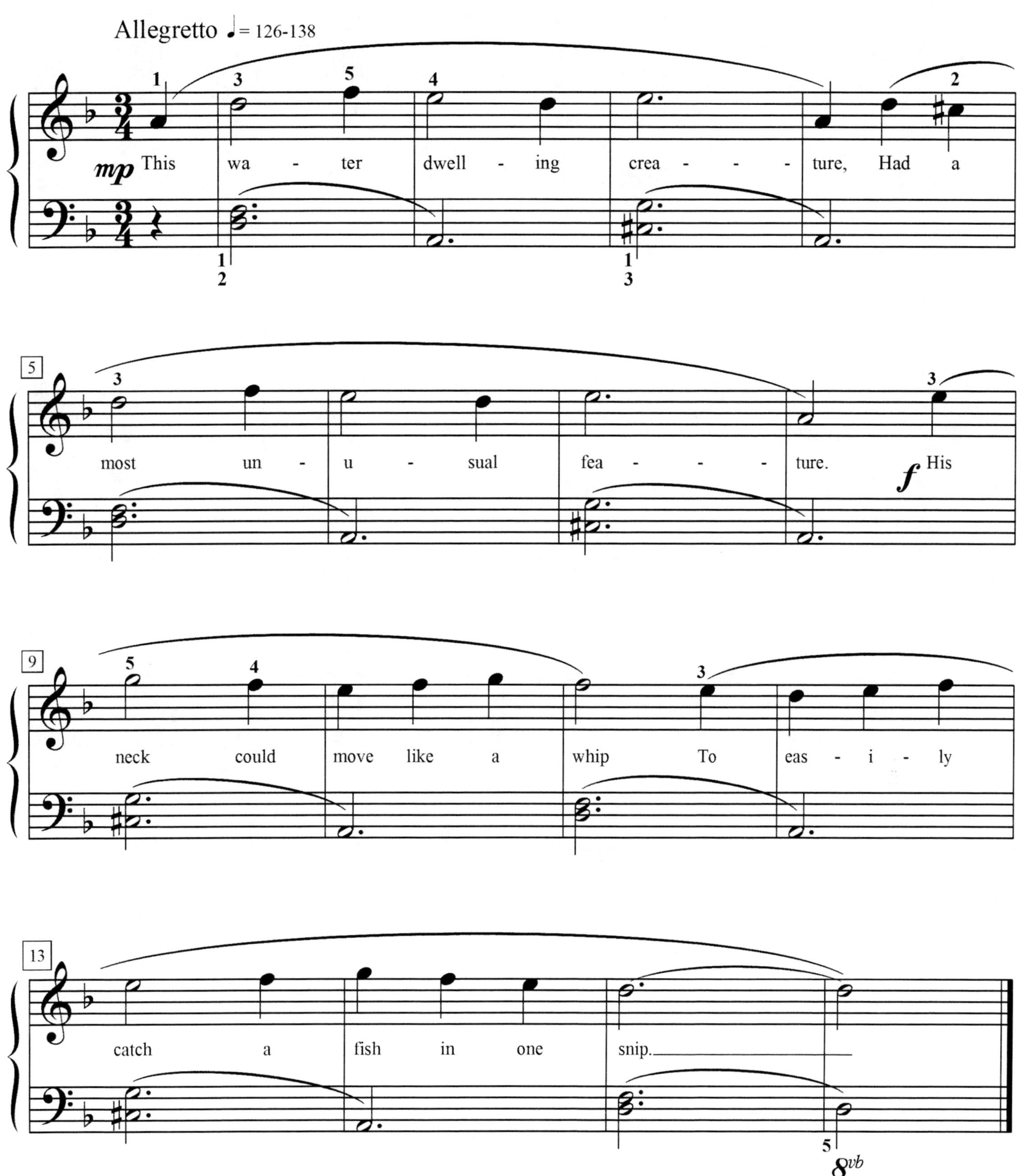

In ancient times, what is now the state of Kansas was covered with water. The **Elasmosaurus** (e-LAS-mo-sawr-us), a sea reptile, has been nicknamed "fish-trap," and rightly so! His body was about 40 feet long, with his head and neck taking up half of its length. Although the elasmosaurus was not a very fast swimmer, his jaws were filled with dagger-like teeth and he could quickly eat fish swimming nearby by whipping around his head and long neck.

Pteranodon

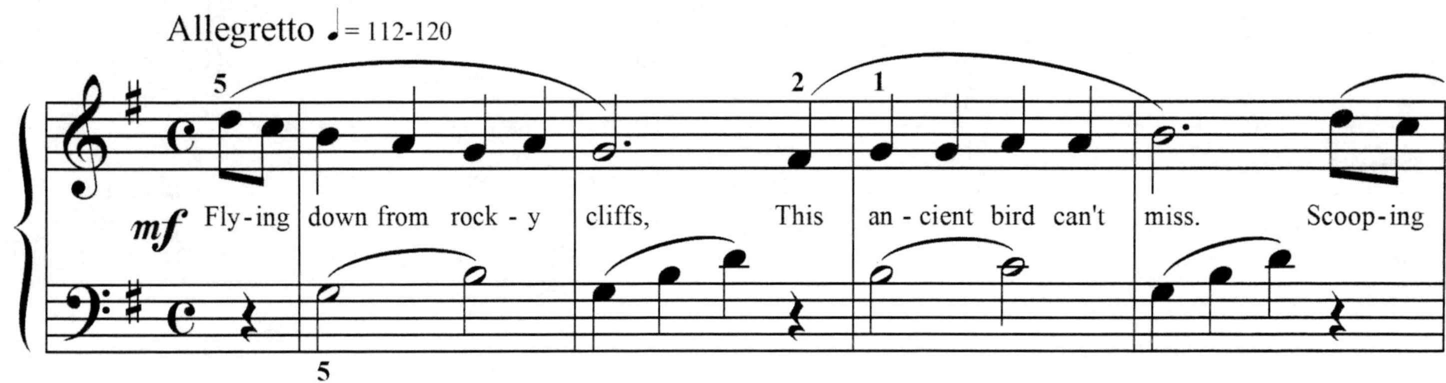

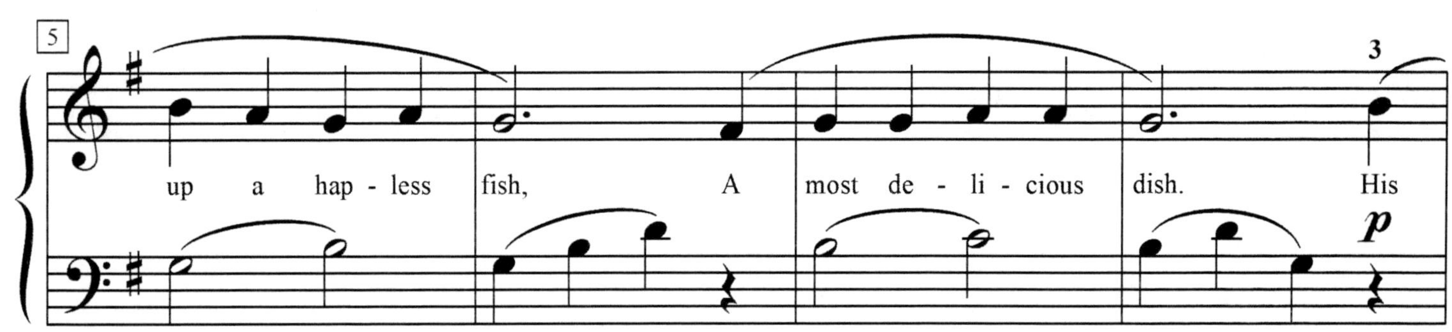

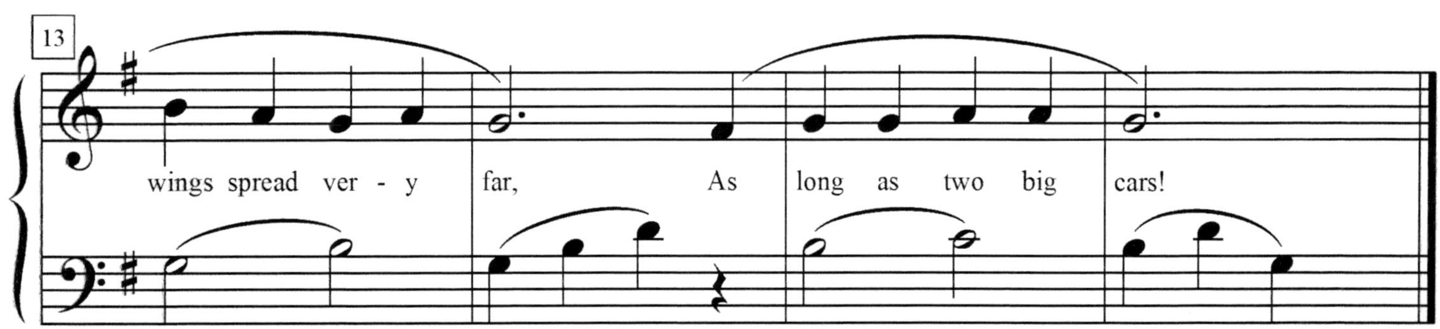

The **Pteranodon** (ter-AN-no-don) lived in ancient cliffs in what is now Texas and Kansas. Its body was roughly the size of a turkey, but it had a wingspan of almost 26 feet! Because of this, scientists think that the pteranodon was a glider rather than a true flyer. The pteranodon had a long, bony crest on the back of its head that may have been used like a rudder, since it had no tail. It also had no teeth, and fed on fish that it snapped up with its beak as it flew over the water, similar to the way pelicans eat.

Dimetrodon

The **Dimetrodon** (di-MEE-tro-don), a "ground lizard" who was as big as a truck, savagely killed large, land-living reptiles in what is now Texas. It had teeth of two different sizes that were very efficient at ripping flesh. It grew to a length of about 10 feet. The large fin on its back was used to regulate its body temperature - absorbing or radiating heat as needed.

Allosaurus

The most vicious flesh-eating dinosaur was the ***Allosaurus*** (al-lo-SAWR-us) who ruled the ancient western lands as the "arch enemy" of all other dinosaurs. It was about 18 feet tall, and 45 feet long. The allosaurus had very powerful legs and was a fast moving, ferocious hunter. The three long toes on its feet were tipped with sharp eagle-like talons. Its jaws were similar to snakes in that they could expand around large portions of its victims.